Don't do a — ny more!" said the

lark!" As

ev ——— 'ry name, And he

led them in -to the ark.

The Bobbs-Merrill Company, Inc.
Publishers   Indianapolis   New York
This illustrated version copyright © 1972, The Felix Gluck Press Limited,
Twickenham. All rights reserved. First published by William Collins Sons &
Company Limited in Great Britain, 1972.
The text in this book is taken from the vocal score of "Captain Noah and His
Floating Zoo," with music by Joseph Horovitz and words by Michael Flanders.
Copyright © 1970, Novello & Company Limited, Borough Green, Sevenoaks,
Kent, England.
Printed in the United States of America
        ISBN 0-672-51841-4
        Library of Congress catalog card number 73-7053
        0 9 8 7 6 5 4 3 2 1

MICHAEL FLANDERS

CAPTAIN NOAH AND HIS FLOATING ZOO

ILLUSTRATED BY HAROLD KING

THE BOBBS-MERRILL COMPANY, INC.
Indianapolis   New York

The Lord looked down on the earth
And it made him sad.
"It should have been good, what I made,
But it turned out bad.
There's nothing but sinning,
Wickedness and violence there.
Remind me to wash Mankind
Right out of my hair!

I'm going to make it rain
And rain and rain!
And then I'll make it rain
And rain again!

Forty days and nights of rain,
I'll wash those sinners
Down the drain!
        Rain and rain
        And rain and rain and rain!

rain rain

"But Noah and his family,
They've been good.
Go, Noah, build me an ark
Of gopher wood.
Four fifty long
By seventy-five feet wide,
And three decks tall, with a roof,
And a door in the side.

I'm going to make it rain
And rain and rain!
And then I'll make it rain
And rain again!

If you want another tip,
Then here you are:
Seal it all up
With a good grade tar:
      Rain and rain
      And rain and rain and rain!

When the ark is finished,
Here's what you do:
Fill it with animals
Two by two.
      Rain and rain
      And rain and rain and rain!

For forty days and forty nights,
There won't be another living soul in sight!
      Rain and rain
      And rain and rain and rain!"

The people of Fun City,
When they could sin no more,
Would go on down to Noah's place
To laugh at poor old Noah.

"You'll never make it float!" they jeered.
"You're miles from any shore.
So God knows what you're doing!"
"He does indeed," said Noah.

"Noah! Noah!
Don't do any more!
Look out man, there's a shark!
Oh ship ahoy there, sailor-boy!"
But he went on building his ark.

Now Shem and Ham and Japhet,
They were the sons of Noah.
He made them get all kinds of food
And lay them in the store.
Said Mrs. Noah, "Ten-thousand buns!
What do we need them for?
Enough to feed an elephant!"
"Enough for *two*," said Noah.

"Noah! Noah!
Don't do any more!
Your boat's a laughing-stock."
But Noah went right on building the ark
And his hammer went knock, knock, knock.

Then Noah told his sons to do
All that the Lord had planned,
To fetch him every kind of thing
That's living on dry land –
The ones you see down on the farm,
The ones you see in zoos –
All reptiles, birds and insects, too,
And line them up in twos.

"Noah! Noah!
Don't do any more!"
The dogs began to bark,
"Just hark at him, old Jungle Jim!"
But he went on building the ark.

Then Japhet, Shem and Ham
Fetched a ewe-sheep and a ram,
Duck and drake and bull and cow and cock and hen,
Male and female spotted cheetahs,
Armadillos and ant-eaters,
And mosquitos and two lions from their den.

All the cats and other felines,
Wombats, walruses and sea-lions,
Hippopotami and spiders and gnus,
Bears and bees and golden eagles,
Horses, harvest-mice and seagulls,
Apes and humming-birds and worms and kangaroos.

All marsupials and mammals,
Such as wallabies and camels,
Snakes and centipedes, a pair of every one.
They got stuck with one giraffe,
Till they found his better half,
Then from antelope to zebra it was done.

Yes, every living creature
That walks upon this earth,
Or creeps upon its belly on the land,
Or flies up in the air,
Just you name it – it was there,
One pair of each, just as the Lord had planned.

"Noah! Noah!
Don't do any more!"
Said the people, "What a lark!"
As creatures came by every name,
And he led them into the ark.

With Mrs. Shem and Mrs. Ham
And Mrs. Japhet, too,
And Mrs. Noah and their husbands four,
They went in two by two.

"Is every living creature there,
Before I shut the door?
Are you all aboard?"
Enquired the Lord.
"We're all aboard!" said Noah.

Noah! Noah!
You can't do any more,
The skies are getting dark.
The Lord will bring you safe to shore,
When you sail away in the ark.

It looks like rain,
Now won't that just be jolly!
It looks like rain,
You know, I thought it would.
It looks like rain,
I must go and get my brolly;
A short, sharp shower
Will do the flowers good.

It looks like rain,
In fact it's really pouring.
It looks like rain,
The ground has turned to mud.
It looks like rain,
Can you hear the river roaring?
I shouldn't be surprised
If it was going to flood!

And now it's round my ankles,
And now it's round my knees,
And some are on the roof-tops
And some are climbing trees.

It looks like the sea
Is rising like a fountain!
It looks like—HELP!
I'm making for the mountain!
It looks like—AAAH!
The world's a brimming jug!
The water's round my shoulders,
And I'm—GLUG!
        GLUG!
          GLUG!

For the flood-gates of Heaven were opened
And the springs of the deep broke through,
And the waters went on rising
As the Lord did command them to.

Then all things living and breathing
On the face of the earth did drown,
For even the peaks of the mountains
Were a good five fathoms down,
Way down,
A good five fathoms down.

But the Lord remembered his promise,
And the ark went floating free,
And the hope of the world went with it
As it sailed on that endless sea.

Forty days and nights
Living under hatches –
Careful with the lights!
Feed the beasts in batches!
And I can't hear them roar
As they're waiting to be fed,
For the rain's steady drumming
On the roof above my head,
The rain-drops drumming overhead.

Forty days at sea –
How the timbers shudder!
God has promised me
He will be our rudder.
But I just can't breathe
And my feet are made of lead,
And the rain's steady drumming
On the roof above my head,
The rain-drops drumming overhead.

Comes another day
Different from the others,
Shem begins to say
Something to his brothers.
But his voice stops short –
There's nothing to be said …

The rain *isn't* drumming
On the roof above my head,
The rain's stopped drumming overhead!

For the Lord closed the flood-gates of Heaven
And the springs of the deep blue sea,
And he sent a West wind blowing
To dry it up gradually.

The waters slowly subsided
Over many long days and weeks,
Till one day they were dotted with islands,
The tips of the mountain peaks,
They were,
The mighty mountain peaks.

The ark went peacefully floating
And the sea was calm and flat,
Till the Lord God brought it to rest at last
On top of Mount Ararat.

Father Noah, please open the porthole,
Let's have a peep at the world outside.
Though we thank the Lord who saved us –
Cain and Abel! What a ride!

Can't believe the ark's not moving,
Are we on a mountain top?
We've come down a whole lot lower,
I just felt my ears go pop!

Let's have a peep through the porthole, Father,
Mother first – then me! Then me!
Mrs. Shem is so very tiny
She can't even see the sea!

Father Noah sent forth a raven,
Flapped around and shouted, "Caw!"
Have another try tomorrow –
Croaked the raven, "Nevermore!"

I can see our tiny island,
Is it really Ararat?
Let me lean out even further…
There goes Mrs. Japhet's hat!

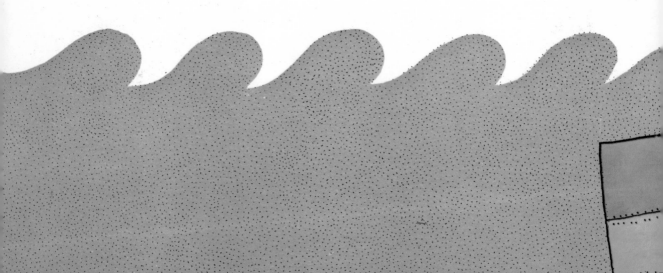

Let's have a peep through the porthole, Father,
Mrs. Ham must have a shot.
"So you boys can see my bloomers?
Thank you, no! I'd rather not!"

Father sent a dove to look-out,
Circled round but found no land.
Then it flew right back through the porthole,
Settled safe on Father's hand.

Sent the dove again a-flying
After waiting for a week.
Back it came that very same evening,
An olive twig held in its beak.

Let's have a peep through the porthole, Father,
Look at what the dove has found!
Where the olive trees are showing,
Soon there's going to be dry ground!

One more week, then off we sent it,
Waited all that day, and then
Sent the other dove to join it;
Neither one came back again.

Now they need no ark for shelter,
There the doves will build their nest,
Where the olive trees are growing,
Make their home and take their rest.

Father Noah, please open the hatches,
Now it must be safe to try –
Gaze about us, blinking in the sunlight,
All the world around is dry!

The Lord looked down on the ark
And he spoke to Noah:
"Come out of the ark
And begin your life once more.
Come out with your wife
And your sons and daughters there,
And set the animals free
And the birds of the air."

And they came out
Two by two
By two by two by two,
Running down the gangplank,
Two by two
By two by two by two.
The Lord said:
"Go where it suits you best
And cover the earth
From East to West,
Two by two
By two by two by two.

"But dog and cat and ox and ass
I give for Noah to keep,
With chicken, turkey, duck and goose
And horse and goat and sheep.

And Man shall sow and till the ground,
And fill it with increase,
While spring shall follow winter round
Until the world shall cease.

Though they do evil in my sight,
I bless the sons of men.
I'll never send another flood
To wipe them out again.

My pledge shall stand between us
As a sign for all to know,
And when the rain-clouds gather,
In the sky I'll set my bow!"

Oh what a wonderful scene–
The rainbow overhead:
Violet, indigo, blue and green,
Yellow, orange and red!

This is God's promise to you–
The rainbow overhead:
Violet, indigo, blue and green,
All the colors that lie between,
Violet, indigo, blue and green,
Yellow, orange and red!

And when you see it in the sky,
You'll know God's words are true:
Go forth, increase and multiply!
By two
    By two
        By two
            By two
                By two
                    By two
                        By two
                            By two
                              By two
                                By two
                                  By two
                                    By two
                                      By two…

By two
   By two
      By two
         By two
            By two
               By two
                  By two
                     By two
                        By two
                           By two
                              By two
                                 By two...